ROAD TRIP

ACKNOWLEDGMENTS

An earlier version of 'Rochelle' was published in *Long Poem Magazine*, autumn 2013.

'An Interview with Comedy Genius Olivier Welsh' was published in *Primers Volume 2* (Nine Arches Press), 2017.

An earlier version of Part 1 of 'The One in Which…' was published in *And Other Poems*, September 2017.

'The Many Reincarnations of Gerald Oswald Archibald Thompson' was published in *Long Poem Magazine*, spring 2018.

'The Baboon Chronicles' was published in *Long Poem Magazine*, summer 2019.

'Cwmcarn' was published in *Bath Magg*, September 2019.

MARVIN THOMPSON

ROAD TRIP

PEEPAL TREE

First published in Great Britain in 2020
Peepal Tree Press Ltd
17 King's Avenue
Leeds LS6 1QS
UK

ISBN 13: 9781845234607

Supported using public funding by
ARTS COUNCIL
ENGLAND

CONTENTS

Part 4

To
Rose Marie Thompson
and
Louis Olivier Thompson

PART 1

THE MANY REINCARNATIONS OF
GERALD OSWALD ARCHIBALD THOMPSON

1. Break a Leg

On the eleventh Christmas Eve
after my dad's death,

I lay awake
reading *Midnight's Children* –

while my son and daughter
snored in their bedroom

(stockings stuffed
with chocolate oranges hanging

from their bunks) –
I saw,

from the corner of my eye,
my dead dad's

bearded face.
Dressed in his maroon

electrician's overalls
with a leather satchel

slung over
his broad shoulders,

he gazed at me
from my wardrobe's

full-length mirror.
Then, he stepped

out of the glass.
In three strides

he was sitting by my cold,
unused pillow.

Slowly, I sat up,
my shaking

calmed
as he traced his rough palm

across my cheek.
Outside,

a helicopter cut
through the dark

as my dad began to talk
about his strange past.

Later, in that night's dream,
I was a mare

galloping too fast
down Ally Pally:

I've never felt more scared
than during that

tumbling.
Sitting on my bed,

my dad looked
oddly relaxed

as he told me,
'My first memory

of serving king
and country

was on a sunny Monday
in Manchester, 1819,

when I charged with my sabre
and slit

three throats.
That manoeuvre

was marred,' he sighed,
'by my horse's

fractured
fibula.'

From his leather bag,
he handed me

two newspaper clippings
as evidence

of his antiquity.
'I've been re-born,'

he told me,
'over and over

as an English soldier.'
As the night marched

into early morning,
my Black dad explained

how he followed
the British military's

bloodiest orders
with a stiff mouth.

2. Dresden

That New Year's Eve,
I sat in front of my TV

trying not to sob
for a father

who was gone when I woke
to drizzle

on Christmas day.
As I tapped my feet

to Dawn Penn
('No, no, no…')

on Jools Holland's
Hootenanny,

I tried to square
my dad's reincarnations

with my Christian beliefs.
By midnight,

my mind was a haze
of spiced rum

and nostalgia:
childhood oaks

in Ally Pally's woods
formed a den,

their branches reaching
for the light.

One August,
the den became

a pretend air-raid shelter
where I munched

bourbon creams
with my bestie Dean.

We imagined blackbirds
were Munich women

praying for the Red Army
to run home

and liberate their gulags
(both Dean and I loved

The World at War
and Sunday servings

of rice and peas).
I'd piss by the birch trees

then clamber into the cockpit
of our Lancaster bomber

(Dean was the gunner).
Sometimes we'd play

at being Danes,
rowing longboats to Iceland

with Irish slaves.
But my memories

have contorted:
the blackbirds sing the din

of Boer children
crammed into the white tents

of concentration camps.
My dad said,

'In that incarnation,
I cleaned the barrel

of my rifle
every night

while children slept
hugging their mother's

jutting ribs.'
His equanimity

seemed like honest madness
until he said:

'I stopped telling God,
Enough's enough

after my thousandth kill.
Now I'm numb

to exit wounds
and limbs

left on beaches.'
Each dawn,

lice and measles spread
in the piss-stinking camps:

a city of scratching
and waiting.

I envisioned mums
who were too thin

to enact the resistance
they planned in their heads;

their daughter's skin
would be creased

by soldiers' hands.
For Boer mothers

that still had strength,
how many cut

their daughter's hair
or read John's Gospel

knowing
there was no Messiah?

3. Dosage

The office fan hummed
and, as instructed,

my dad filled
the syringe

with too much morphine.
Under Aden's sun,

he ignored the sobs
and fed the needle

into the prisoner's arm.
Telling the story,

Dad chuckled.
On my honeymoon,

John crows circled
St. Lucia's dusk

and Aden swam
into my mind:

why did my dad tell me
about these crimes

after his death?
'When I was first stopped

by the police,'
he said, 'in my XR3i,

I readied my tongue
(patois became plum)

and wound the window.
Then I raised my hands

as Bach rose
from my radio –

I was going to tell them,'
he said, chuckling some more,

'that I know what it's like
to prey on darkies.'

Now I drink Red Stripe
to forget

not being on hand
to hold his thinning frame

as his nurse increased
his dose.

4. Eat your Heart Out

When cancer consumed
his prostate,

Dad left his life
in Millennial London.

I want to ask him
if he remembers

each family
or if his soul's

descent
into other bodies

is predetermined.
He told me

about his journey
through time

because he knew
no one would believe me.

That Christmas dawn,
I awoke

and strolled downstairs,
eyes in a swirl of tears:

the front door mat
was sprinkled

with icing sugar
to mimic North Pole snow;

Rudolph's carrot
was half-eaten

and my dad was gone.
He left a clipping

for verification –
an Oxo advert

from 1943.
It took me two years

to free myself
from uncertainty

and believe
my memories;

sometimes I'm cool
with the fact

that his hands
and his aftershave's scent

have gone.
Then my thoughts flow

to the Bengal famine
he witnessed –

I want my version of him
alive

so he can seek redemption
sitting in the pew

beside me.
Maybe his soul

has been rehoused
in Helmand

or wherever
British soldiers stand

with their trousers down
in front of

squirming bodies.
Perhaps he's tearing

through the Falklands
in a Harrier

or on a plantation
where he's chasing men,

bayonet ready,
into Jamaica's

misty hills.
I scroll

through Wikipedia's
famine page

while munching granola.
A Bengali girl

looks up from my screen
with smallpox sores

covering her face.
Her body

is every human body.
This morning, Dad,

the Christmas drizzle
is back,

my garden's
plum tree branches

look black
and my love for you

feels doomed.

PART 2

THE ONE IN WHICH…

1. The one in which my children discuss jazz while we set out to watch *The Lego Batman Movie* in Blackwood

A crow rises into the morning mizzle as mist clings to the valley.
Tired, I bark at my five-year-old Derys to 'Focus'
on her seatbelt. She cries. I wipe mucus from her top lip

and tell her there's liquorice in my rucksack. She kicks my bag.
Hayden (aged six) shouts, 'This music's angry!'
On alto sax, Joe Harriott's abstract jazz swirls around us.

'Sad and crazy!' snaps Derys. We fall into silence.
As I drive, a smile curls – my Mixed Race children are listening
to something I want them to love: art that sings

Africa's diaspora and raises skin to radiance.
But they haven't asked to learn a history of defiance
or the blues' dark beauty. Is this upbringing

or brainwashing? Below the grey-green hills in Hafodyrynys,
Hayden asks, 'Does the trumpet sound like a forest fire or an arrest?'
My best mate's mixtapes melted during the policing protest

that blazed on Broadwater Farm. Should we tour the bliss
and sadness those high-rises hold for me? 'Where we live's not racist,'
I was once warned. Cymbals shimmer. A loneliness rests.

2. The one in which I drive through Crumlin wondering where the cigarette-razed crisp factory used to be

Despite its tileless roof and its weeds, there is an iridescence
to Crumlin's crumbling colliery. Except, this morning as I cruise
beyond its towering chimney, I imagine its bruising

underworld – the scent of dust and sweat silenced
like this valley's churches. I change gear as if in the presence
of ghosts. In her Grenfell bedroom, with smoke crawling,

would my Derys cwtch her teddies or her Barbies?
In my vision, I lie by her door as carbon monoxide lines
my lungs. The gas won't be confined;

assisted by cladding, it spreads over neighbours sleeping
in front of TVs. I picture my Hayden nodding awake
like a coal mine trapper who'd sit alone for hours as methane seeped

from the coal seam. From Grenfell's 23rd floor, a son's *Goodbye* sailed
in a Snapchat. The roadside willows look weary.
Derys asks: 'Are my sandwiches Marmite?' 'Sorry,'

I reply, wondering why I made her ham. Hayden yells: 'Epic fail!'
Grenfell lacked sprinklers – cost-cutting prevailed.
In my mind, Derys runs down its storeys. Her slippers are soggy.

3. The one in which we travel 30m above the Sirhowy River

Mountain clouds clench like a Maroon's fists
as she sleeps beyond sugarcane and soldiers' guns with her sons
and daughters in Jamaica's hills – fists like Jack Johnson's,

an 18th Century Haitian's or an ANC activist's.
Rain falls knuckle-hard on the giant arms of a brass Chartist.
Crossing Blackwood's bridge, I wonder at what age I'll hand Hayden

and Derys *The History of Mary Prince,* the slave memoir I stole
from school in Year 8. That dusk, slurping Dad's spag bol,
I read; in Bermuda's heat, I hunched over with Mary. We raked salt

from a saltpond, brine biting through our bare legs, shin bones
exposed. Will my fury be passed on to my children? Will it be easy
to explain why Chartists marched, demanding suffrage for all

men and not women? From the stereo, Joe Harriott's alto tone hints
at calypso and conjures iron mined with calloused hands,
iron used to forge oil barrels and steel pans

that echo Kaiso. By the road, wet beeches rise dark as flint
and the clouds hold an ominous tint;
the first flakes of spring snow fall, ready to suffocate the land.

4. The one in which I recall standing in the cinema's cream-coloured foyer procrastinating over Häagen-Dazs

My tongue's been stung with pangs for Wray and Nephews white –
rum my dead Jamaican dad poured with joy over Cornish ice-cream.
Yesterday, as I indulged, the scent of his cinema liquorice

seemed to rise into the evening, Derys dancing to 'She's Royal', the voice
of Tarrus Riley a sweet gruffness. On the big screen, noonlight
cascades: Rihanna's makeup advert opens to a gull's flight

above a cityscape; there's a sheen to the folds of a young woman's hijab
and another woman's cheeks hold an onyx darkness.
Kerbs and car horns cut to luminous office blocks,

freckled shoulders and St. Lucian-blue eyeshadow. The ad's bass jabs
and I imagine Dad crooning, 'Ride, cowboy, ride...' as Hayden dabs.
My feet fizz with a sense of Caribbeanness;

a Barbadian is selling foundation to my daughter
and her White friends. Mainstream marketing is targeting melanin!
One day, I'll tell Derys that I hoped she'd have Afro hair, the combing

and cane-rows – rites I would've held her hands through. Should I be happier
that she fits into her White Welsh world? The film starts; chatter
fades as my children munch Butterkist. Here it is: the scent of liquorice.

WHILST SEARCHING FOR ANANSI WITH MY MIXED RACE CHILDREN IN THE BLAEN BRAN COMMUNITY WOODLAND

1.

A fox lies still by a birch. 'Dad, is it dead?'
asks Derys. Crouching down, I watch an ant
crawl through its ear-fur. Inside my head

are Mark Duggan's smile and last night's heavy dread:
I dreamt his death again. A distant love
once stroked my cheek and said: *'They shot him dead*

only because he had a gun.' I still see red
and white carnations; a girl who now frequents
her father's grave; brown birch leaves descending

a walk to school. '85. Mum's palm bled
sweat, Tottenham's air strangely grey. Stagnant.
We passed my friend's burnt front door – flames had fed

on parked cars. In tower blocks, rage had spread
like an Arab Spring: numbing unemployment,
the oppressive use of sus laws. *'Is my friend dead?'*

Mum answered with silence. Hunkered on mud,
my prayer withers, the birch's leaves hang slant
and noonlight shrouds the fox. 'Sorry. It's dead.'
'It's breathing, Dad,' shouts Hayden. 'Listen, hard!'

2

Crouched by the fox's nose, I listen
to placate my son. The fox is breathing.
Should I leave it here to die? Its fur glistens

with drizzle – each breath makes my eyes moisten
as though a gospel singer's voice is rising
from the fox's lungs. Derys blurts, 'Dad, listen,

it needs a vet!' In the dream, Mark Duggan
lay on the Gold Coast's shore, smoke soaring
above ancestors whose dark necks glistened,

chains ready on docked ships from London.
I woke, limbs tensed, ancestors' rage jumping
in my blood, the humid night laden

with sailors screams: *'Masts ablaze!'* Will Britain
learn to love my children's melanin?
With their voices ('Yellow bird, high up…') swelling,

I carry the limp fox. The grey mountains
are watching us. A buzzard's circling.

I scratch and scratch my wrists. The vet stiffens,
holding her stethoscope. The fox's eyes listen.

CWMCARN

I lie outside
the glamping pod

in the scent
of dog rose

as starlings
rise and rise

into dusk's reds.
The distant

sound
of a siren

seems as strange
as the caravan

I saw in a field
rusting

on last week's
Blaen Bran

woodland walk.
Having read

twelve pages
of Maggie

Aderin-Pocock's
biography

to Derys and a now
snoring Hayden,

my gut
feels heavy

with guilt
for not finding

a book about
a Mixed Race

scientist
for my

Mixed Race
children.

The horizon's
hills

are a patchwork
of mud;

to halt
disease,

150,000 larches
have been

felled. I imagine
the industrial

saws, the fumes,
the new

brambles' fruit
(our fingers

will be stained
with our first

blackberrying).
I hear deer grunting

like the fenced deer
I used to visit

in Ally Pally
as a lonely

Year 7.
As the bucks ate,

I'd pretend
that if

I touched
their antlers

I'd assuage
my confusion:

born in London,
was I English

like school's
niggers out

graffiti?
Did my parents

make me Jamaican?
Or was I,

by ancestry,
African?

In my mind,
the deer

multiply
and stand

in this clearing,
breath

to breath.
On my phone,

I re-watch
my favourite

cage fighter's
throat-

choked
defeat. His tears

are the same tears
I swallowed

when a taxi driver
on a Kingston

roadside
branded me,

my parents,
my brothers

English.
Not Jamaican.

What if
Derys and Hayden

choose
to identify

as White
in a Britain

that will call them
Black?

The sky
darkens.

On YouTube,
I forego

Oliver Samuels
and belly laughs

to watch
the slowing

of seconds
as Les Twins

dance.

PART 3

ROCHELLE

1. Reading Services

At the table, Rochelle watched brown sugar fall
into her coffee's froth. Her legs were shaking,
opposite the hitchhiker's bearded scowl.

Rochelle sipped, each second as slow as withdrawal.
'My mum,' she stuttered, 'is always talking
about me moving back to Pontypool

which would make her happy and…' the downward curl
of the hitchhiker's mouth grew more pronounced.
Rochelle bit into her cold bacon roll

and chewed its blandness. Spring's 5 A.M. squall
was rising. In truth, there wasn't an ounce
of Rochelle that wanted to leave Wales

but there she was, part way to Winchmore Hill,
London, to see her sister. The hitchhiker?
She hadn't even asked him his name. The call

was what really weighed on her mind, the pull
of words: 'I've had a miscarriage' – *my sister
not gloating for once.* 'I'll come see you, girl.'

2. Monument

Rochelle approached the Chiswick roundabout
close to tears: *Turn back, this is a waste of time,*
I can't cwtch her or listen to her bullshit.

The air was heavy with the threat of sleet;
it felt like the old days when she'd do a line
of coke or speed to keep her sharp, alert

during 3 A.M. revision, her heart
buoyed by the fact she was outperforming
her sister. Rochelle had fought her parents

then acquiesced – she read physics, not art. The hate
she had for her sister was now trickling
down her face, her tears thick and salty and hot.

Behind her, her passenger was still silent.
'We met two hours ago and you've said
two words to me? Weird. You'll have to get out

at Hangar Lane.' She was on a side street
trying to work her way to the main road
when she saw something strange caught in her headlights.

3. A Beech-Lined Street

Rochelle pulled over. *Is this a dream?*
Lit by her main beam, a chestnut horse walked
towards her car, its eyes like dark gems;

then it stopped. Three feet away. Like a bloom
in a desert. On the radio, Björk:
her voice, the harp, the violins were somehow warm

and bleak. In that moment, her sister, Blossom,
was twelve, locking Rochelle under the stairs
while Dad was out screwing someone who wasn't Mum

and Mum was working nights as a locum.
Rochelle remembers the school yard, spitting: *'Jug ears,
jug ears,'* as Blossom sobbed and Rochelle's friends swarmed

and laughed with her. There was a strange rhythm
to the reggae song now on the radio.
She heard one of the car doors open: the hum

of distant traffic rushed in; the door slammed
and the horse reared. In the headlights' glow
the hitchhiker was stroking the horse, calm.

4. Road Block

The mare gave a short neigh, its withers
muscular under Rochelle's touch. 'She's smiling.
She likes you more than me,' said the hitchhiker.

Rochelle grinned: 'Fun fact about my sister –
she lives on a street called Broad Walk.' 'No kidding?'
Silence. Then Rochelle started to whisper:

'Oh when the sun beats down and burns the tar
up on the roof…' The hitchhiker joined in
and their voices rose. As Rochelle danced, the night air

held their song's last note, let it linger.
The hitchhiker said, 'I can't keep my flat clean
and I'm going to be my mum's carer.

God's taking the piss. She'll be up now, at her Aga
frying dumplings, jerk chicken and plantain.
But give her about half an hour

and she won't know where she is.' 'Hello there!'
someone said – the voice urgent. A torch beamed
and Rochelle saw a man holding horse gear.

5. Archway

'How'd you get the nickname Kite?' Rochelle asked.
The Hangar Lane gyratory fell back
into the distance and the dawn sky was a hard

grey-red. 'I used to smoke tons of weed,' Kite said.
'I thought that's what you did if you were Black.'
Rochelle glanced at him, knowing she'd found a friend

as broken as her. Someone who'd understand
how she felt about seeing her sister. 'My mum
used to work near here,' Kite said. He sighed:

'She was a psychiatric nurse. As a child,
I didn't get why she was always glum
and shouty. After forty years, she retired

and guess what? She almost got deported
because of that Windrush shit.' In his silence
and rage, Rochelle sensed his need to be held;

for a moment she wanted to be kissed
by him. Tired, they arrived at the entrance
of Kite's mum's house. The garage opened.

6. The Lounge

'Says he's going to do a Morgan Freeman.'
Kite's mum smiled. 'Actors his age only play Lear!'
She plunged the cafetiere. 'I'm Suzanne.'

On the walls, a large Basquiat and a Cézanne –
Mont Sainte Victoire – sent Rochelle back to the years
when a sketch pad was always in her hands.

The fragrance of ackee and cayenne
drifted in from the Aga. 'When you save,'
Suzanne smiled, 'this house is what happens. And…

my sister used to tease me and call me *Sly-Anne*.
Getting dressed for school, I'd tell her, *Go shave
your moustache!* I would've played Chopin

at her funeral, but she requested Bach.
In the end, I didn't know my sister and that hurts.'
Outside, the rain stopped. Rochelle hugged Suzanne

as she sat at her piano. When she rang
her sister, Rochelle felt a dryness in her throat.
'I'll stay at yours,' she said and love sang, sang, sang.

THE WEIGHT OF THE NIGHT

1. After the Stag Do

As the evening dims, Lisa stares out of your white-tiled kitchen. June rain is drumming the conservatory roof. You fix your eyes on your cornflakes, scared that if you talk, your secret will pour out of you. Last night, as you danced, you felt something akin to a spiritual joy. You wish those moments were now. You spoon and peer at your cereal. Lisa asks, 'Apart from you downing a skinful, what else happened?' You don't want to reply but the question hangs. Silence: it's as though your words are stones in your throat and your blood is jittering. 'I did something bad,' you tell Lisa and look out at the downpour. Lisa's face is a mix of love and fear. Your wet tabby paws at the window. Lisa lets him in, and sits next to you. Her perfume is a soft wall between you. You look at the sink then stutter: 'Once, when I was younger, I had sex without proper consent.' Somewhere, rain pounds a prison courtyard. 'Not funny,' Lisa says. As she speaks, a spot of her spit lands on your trembling lip. She lets out a chuckle: 'Two weeks before our wedding? Are you trying to...' From her chair, she steps backwards, reading the despair on your face. As her eyes moisten, you imagine the first raindrop that starts a monsoon that leads to mothers lying on roadsides. 'It was my ex, Sara,' you say. In the conservatory, the cat rolls one of its toys – a ball with a bell. 'You should phone her.' 'She'd hang up.' With her back against the fridge, Lisa's eyes sear into your face. You try to explain: 'At night,' you say, staring at your bowl, 'Sara and I had a regular game. She'd pretend to be asleep while I woke her up by... And... one night, when she turned round, she didn't smile. She looked alarmed. I told myself she was acting. We never talked about it.' The rain slows. Out of the silence, Lisa says, 'Find her on Facebook. Message her. I need to know that she forgives you.'

2. Pendine Beach

Alone, you stroll the dawn sand picturing Lisa's smile. Above the distant sea, a tern glides, then swoops downwards, out of sight. In three hours, you would have been shining your wedding shoes and sipping spiced rum. The air's driftwood scent reminds you of your first holiday kiss in the black of a post-disco walk. Back then, you didn't know that love could make your lungs ache. You listen to the coastline's quiet as if you're listening to Lisa talk about *Moonlight,* or any film she adores. The sea stretches itself across the horizon. In last night's dream, its waves were black. You stood in them, scoffing wedding cake. A ragged breeze rises. You sit on the damp sand, hugging your knees. Your phone vibrates. Sara is calling. In the distance, someone is jogging with a large dog. You wonder what scent is used to teach hounds to chase foxes and tear their bodies into a bloody mess. Lisa said: 'I'm glad Sara's moved on. I can't.' The jogger bears down on your patch of beach, her doberman bounding. You pull your phone from your jeans pocket. 'I've bought a new bed,' Sara says. 'I couldn't sleep in the one you'd laid in.' In your throat, your pulse thuds. 'After we talked last week,' she says, 'I wrote things down. Eleven years ago, in my bedroom, you didn't care enough about consent to stop. Do you know what I see when I look at our old selfies? Me with a rapist.' You're sent back to that night – light from her landing crawling over her sheets, the blunt scent of your sweat. You open your dry mouth and offer: 'I thought–' 'We used to pray to be better Christians,' Sara says and you want the sea to wail and drown out the anguish in her voice. She sobs: 'When you put the phone down, walk into the nearest police station and confess.' Her words are whirring in your head. The cloying scent of wedding cake icing leaks from last night's dream where hushing waves wrapped their oily blackness around your thighs. Your breath is short, short and in this tumbling sunshine you can't breathe. 'Go to the police or I will.' Gazing at the distant sea, you hang up. You walk towards the sea wall. There is a scrap of black bin bag dancing in the breeze. Again, you inhale the smell of driftwood. You stare back at the waves. In your car, you can only look down.

PART 4

AN INTERVIEW WITH COMEDY GENIUS
OLIVIER WELSH

1. When did you first know you wanted to be a stand-up comic?

'The sun has got his hat on. Hip. Hip. Hip,'
is what Gramps drawled during drives to sea air
where throats were eased from hayfever's rough grip.
Those days kicked off by Gramps' Art Deco leer;
in shorts and Yankees cap he'd yawn or scowl
and switch from Dad's dub to Radio 3.
Then in old Jamaican patois he would howl:
'Watch the road. Stop trying to kill me!'

The taunting tone was a game for us three;
how long could we cork up our wild cackling?
I'd mimic Gramps till our Adam's apples jigged.
'You'll be a stand-up star,' Gramps said hoarsely.
I'd smell his grave's rain-wet soil, wondering
if I'd one day honour him with Vegas gigs.

2. Was it difficult to turn your back on all the drugs?

Syringe in hannd after an O_2 gig
and with my lipstick wiped into a tearful smear,
I sat on the loo floor, veins fat as pigs.
Gramps' smoking jacket lay still as stale beer.

I drifted to Chestnut Farm's sweaty chores,
cows farting their methane into the air.
Sharon's eyes shone like Diana Dors'
and made our Year 10 work experience less austere,

clearing a path to summer's Dizzee songs,
uni, and that winter when we froze
in our first bedsit. That's where I let love wane,

my nights spent rehearsing jokes. 16 years on
her Facebook page lit that loo: *Pete proposed!*
How could I flush the stuff that numbed my pain?

3. What's the truth about how Tommy Mann was born?

2016 was a year of pain,
'Muslims go home!' spat from once-shy mouths.
Like Enoch Powell, Brexit turned tongues profane.
We were not so much divided by north and south
but by politicians' poisonous, post-truth views.
Have I Got News For You hosted my protest
of ironic racist quips in Gramps' royal blue,
a jacket Tommy wore with a puffed chest.

Tommy's first pub gig? I choked with fright.
His smoking jacket dripped with punters' spit
and his barbs about refugees' bums were booed.
So I studied, gave his voice more plum, more bite
and learnt his swagger: Tommy's path was lit.
To date on YouTube? Nine billion views.

4. What are your thoughts on comedians using the N-word?

There's a documentary with only nine views
that explains how the N-word spawned from a need
to dehumanise people of a dark hue
so cotton profits would feel less like greed

or sin. The word's history is not well known.
Its US uses are born from complex battles
but when it's packaged as an endearment I groan:
it still points to people owned as cattle.

But with Richard Pryor, 'nigger' assumed beauty
which gave high fives to civil rights and shame.
Like joking about his own heart attack,

it gave him scope to poke fun brutally
at a land where folk sing Christ whilst crosses flame.
Compared to Pryor, all my jokes fall flat.

5. Which British comedians do you admire?

With Felix Dexter, even my jokes clap!
Yet he represents my heart's ambivalence.
From St Kitts to Slough – his gigs reeked of wet beer mats.
I'd watch his *Real McCoy* on VHS.
Mum's dusty tapes crackled with my first crush
and gave the air a Caribbeanness
that made me see my Sharon's lips as lush.

But what happened to the rich, ragamuffin accents
and the sweet segregation of Auntie's airwaves
that gave voice to Black stand-ups that nose dived?
Do Sky tell jokes about hair relaxants?
Where's the *Kumars'* equivalent on Dave?
I mimicked White males on TV and thrived!

6. But isn't it true that you've been influenced *artistically* by a host of White comedians?

By mimicking white men my career's thrived.
My Oxbridge Bernard Manning – what wild japes!
But to joke about John crows and Brixton's Hive
that once served Sharon's patties and salted hake?

What's in the hearts of families that spoon
black bean sauce and beef on our high streets
then call the chefs Cs (and I don't mean 'coons'
which is Tommy's word for 'Lives we should delete.')

I digress. It's true, Izzard wore slap and soared
with better gags and nails and cuter heels.
With me, who knows why the world is enthralled?

Tommy's tales are Corbett to the core.
Maybe then, the truth's just been revealed:
the Black part of me's not funny at all.

7. Tell us about the controversy surrounding your hosting of the Oscars

Two years ago, I watched my bright skies fall
after ranting about Saint Obama's death.
Parliament announced they were appalled
while Black activists denounced my very breath.
My management told me, 'Soften your quips,
or forget Vegas.' I gave in. Tommy raged
and turned to warpaint: rouged cheeks, rib-white lips.
In thigh-high boots, he stomped across each stage.

I found out six months late: Sharon had died.
I pleaded, 'Pull me from the Oscars job.'
In pain, I left my pen in Tommy's grip;
his wrath was a mask behind which I cried.
The Oscars aired – Tommy, in blackface, gobbed:
'The sun has got his hat on. Hip. Hip. Hip.'

THE BABOON CHRONICLES

Stephen:

You smile at me on my doorstep, invite me round your house for
     drinks,
then ask me to recount my dealings with the boys in blue?
Do you also extend this the kind of hospitality to your new White
     neighbours?
No wonder the estate agent kept banging on about this street being
     'baboon
quiet.' It's the only – No, I'm leaving and no, I don't need coffee, I
     live across the road.
Actually, wait. Here's a story for you. It was a Saturday morning,

about a month ago. You know, one of those spiteful mornings
that seems to promise rain but just gets hotter and hotter. I was
     drinking
an Earl Grey while stood on dust sheets – my bathroom looked like
     a desert road.
Having sanded the walls, I was ready to paint my first coat of ash blue.
Then I remembered that I'd lost my cutting-in brush. Outside, the
     baboons
were into their braying, one of the fat males baring its off-white teeth

to a female. I drove to the Screwfix in Pontnewynydd, the sky bone
     white.
Halfway to the industrial estate, the traffic stopped and the morning's
sticky heat closed in on me. I could picture it: a brute of a baboon
hunched over in the middle of the carriageway, drinking in
the pleasure of its ticks being picked while enraged drivers turned
     the air blue.
As I inched past a bus stop, I noticed one of the monkeys was sat
     roadside

grinning at me, its teeth like blades. Oh, the irony – the bus-stops
        down that road
are all plastered with posters telling us to, 'Vote YES for the cull!'
        The whites
of the primate's eyes were murky, there was a blueness
to its face as if it was sick and it was swaying on the kerb, the morning
growing ever more sweaty and oppressive. Yep, it was drunk!
I agree, you must be vermin to leave bowls of liquor for baboons

to lap up. I've seen this video where men are laughing while feeding
        baboons
gin from baby bottles on one of those desolate, coastal roads.
Anyway, by the time I reached Screwfix, I was vexed and in need of
        a drink
of camomile and honey. The store was empty apart from the two
        White women
behind the counter. Browsing the Argos-style catalogue gave
        the morning
a sense of calm, but I soon sensed the ladies' eyes crawling over me,
        all blue-rinse

and rage. Their skin evoked Britain's colonial past and something
        in me blew.
I approached the counter. The shorter lady, wearing a red 'Baboons
        out!'
wrist band, snarled: 'Suzi, you serve him.' Like a man in angry
        mourning,
my pulse thumped and thumped, howling seeping in from the road.
Suzi reached out and I passed her my order slip, her hair a lank,
        greasy white.
She toyed with a computer then disappeared into the warehouse –
        for drinks?

She took that long, my temper grew: 'This is not the morning
for drunk White women to –' 'Shut up, you 'boon!' My fists rolled,
       hard as a road.
A millisecond from diving over the counter, I heard someone clear
       their throat
behind me. A police officer stood by the door, baton in hand.
       Grinning.

Sally:

Pastor, the chemo isn't working and I'm so tired all the time; it's as
     if I'm drunk.
At night, I can't sleep. I feel the cancer eating my bowels and the white
of my bones. Sometimes I listen to my husband's records, especially
     the blues
he recorded with BB King. When I'm woken by the howling baboons,
I watch them from my bedroom window. Some look as scrawny as
     roadkill
and I long for my husband, my dear dead Sam. I long for the morning

when I am with him again. But I'm scared. I'm still in mourning
over what he did ten years ago, something so sinful that I could drink
and keep drinking until I'm numb. It happened in June, 2000, when
     our road
was baboon quiet. We slept in separate rooms – his snoring was like
     white noise!
When he was in hospital, he told me how he almost hit a baboon
as he drove to Llandegfedd Reservoir's deserted car park. The moon
     was blue,

he said, and he sat shaking in his Porsche, thinking about the quiet
     blue
of the reservoir's water and our granddaughter, Suzi. She was 18. Her
     morning sickness
had kicked in and she'd vomit buckets and howl like a baboon
in our guest room (her mum kicked her out again). I'm sure she was
     drinking
while pregnant. The first time he took her windsurfing, Wales was
     white
with springtime snow. I thought he was mad. 'What about the roads?'

I protested. 'I'll take the Land Rover,' he said. He told me that she
rode
the water like she was born for it. It became their thing. Under that
blue moon,
years after Suzi abandoned windsurfing, Sam let the beaming white
of his torch lead him to the reservoir's edge. He'd filled his morning
flask
with his favourite Penderyn single malt. He looked out at the water,
drinking,
and thinking about our Suzi. 'The rucksack on my back was heavy as
a 'boon,'

he said. It was full of bricks. Suzi used to collect pebbles, dark as
runes
and call them mermaid's tears. They'd go on long trips down coastal
roads
and she'd win competitions. She loved it. She also caught him when
he was drunk
and dancing in his garage to Johnny Cash wearing a basque and blue
heels.
'£200 a week and I'll keep schtum.' His reply? 'Just don't tell Sal.'
By morning,
he'd handed her the first payment. I knew he liked wearing my lacy
whites.

I should have told him that I didn't care. In the months that followed,
there was a whiteness
to his skin: he was scared that I'd find out, treat him like some sick
baboon
and leave him. Plus the money and the lies. He stopped waking me
for morning cwtches
and one night he found himself by the res. He once told me,
'Sometimes, all roads
lead to sin.' He walked into the water depressed and I couldn't stop
the night's blue
engulfing him. He raised his flask in salute to God and took a long
drink.

Out of the dark, a baboon wild for liquor leapt onto his face, tearing
 at the white
of his teeth, his tongue. The next morning, I sat by his hospital bed,
 drinking
black coffee from Suzi's blue thermos while she shed her crocodile
 tears. Pastor,
for what Sam attempted, he's in hell. After our talk, I'm ready to walk
 that road.

Suzi:

Nana Sally, I've never told you this, so excuse me, but I'm going to drink
at your grave to steady myself. I was 18 and awake at silly o'clock feeling blue
about my pregnancy. I was in your guest room, my belly big as a white moon,
needing to pee again but not wanting to wake anyone. I felt like a baboon.
I was ugly and unwanted. In dreams, I'd walk down a deserted road
to a blood-red sea. Eventually, I heaved myself out of bed knowing that the morning

would bring vomit and a sense of doom. The previous morning,
Gramps had bought himself a new toy: a Porsche. After taking a drink
of water, I thought I'd have a peep at his car, remembering the roads
that took us to windsurfing competitions and service station chocolate, the blues
soaring from Gramps' speakers. I wanted to stroll into traffic like a loon,
get hit and bleed out. But I had a boy coming. At your garage's white door,

I stood still, scared. The foot of the door was leaking white light.
There were footsteps inside. I knew you and Gramps would be in bed till morning.
Burglars? My womb quaked. Then I experienced a wave of baboon-like
bravery. Surely, any intruder, high on drugs or drink
would take one look at my enormous belly and refrain from leaving me blue
with bruises. Or maybe they'd shoot me dead. Both were roads

I was happy to take, so I opened the garage door. At the time, I was
        making slow inroads
into my debts and the father of my child told me he'd slap the white
from my eyes if I went through with the birth. In the soft blue light
of the garage, Gramps was dancing like he was at Carnival, the
        morning
and the night one long expanse of love. I felt almost drunk
with joy. He was wearing a black basque and heels the colour of a
        harvest moon.

I'm scum for what I did when he spun round. He looked as shocked
        as a baboon
shot between the eyes. He once told me, 'Sometimes, all roads
lead to sin.' I whispered, '£200 a week and I'll keep schtum,
        you old drunk.'
I started to sweat with regret. Gramps just begged me not to tell you,
        his face ash-white.
After what happened at the res, I ran up north to Hull. That first
        morning,
for all my sin, I couldn't eat or pray. Things I did up there would turn
        your teeth blue.

But my little Emyr. He's in London studying jazz piano. He says
        Gramps played the blues
like he was from Mississippi. He messages me about his love life and
        the baboon
he secretly feeds in his garden. I'd still be in Hull except there was
        this spring morning,
about three years ago. I was sat in a park, recalling these cold Welsh
        roads
and sobbing. I had to come back. And here I am with all the white
        roses
that you'd love. Don't worry, I've pulled the weeds. I'd offer you a
        drink

but... Hey, about a month ago, a Black guy came into my store. Kim
   called him a 'boon –
she's a morning drunk – I dialled 999 – their yelling was turning the
   air blue
and Kim had a hammer under the counter. An officer came in off the
   road and calmly asked:
'Who wants to borrow my baton?' There was silence. Then the guy
   just walked out.

ABOUT THE AUTHOR

Marvin Thompson was born in Tottenham, north London to Jamaican parents. He now teaches English to secondary school children in mountainous south Wales. This debut collection is a Poetry Book Society Recommendation.

In 2019, he was one of only eight writers to be awarded a grant by Literature Wales as part of the Platforming Under-Represented Writers Funding Scheme. His war poem, 'The Many Reincarnations of Gerald Oswald Archibald Thompson' was submitted by *Long Poem Magazine* for the 2019 Forward Prize for Best Poem. In addition, 'The One in Which' and 'The Weight of the Night' were shortlisted for the 2019 Manchester Poetry Prize.

As well as having an MA in Creative Writing, Thompson was selected by Nine Arches Press for the Primers 2 mentoring scheme. Reviewers of the anthology described his work as 'exciting', 'dramatic' and 'a virtuoso performance'.